Room for God

In affectionate memory of Danny Harrison
whose child-like faith was an integral part of his daily life.

Room for God

Anne Evans

National Society/Church House Publishing

National Society/Church House Publishing
Church House
Great Smith Street
London SW1P 3NZ

ISBN 0 7151 4871 0

Published 1996 by The National Society and Church House Publishing

© *The Central Board of Finance of the Church of England* 1996

Printed in England by the Longdunn Press Ltd

God bless the place where I live;
give blessing to all that it holds.

O God bless the journeys I make;
give blessing to travel and rest.

O God bless the words that I speak;
give blessing to silence and talk.

O God shield my heart from guilt;
fill our bodies and spirits with joy.

O God bless the folk I live with;
give blessing to our livelihood.

O God let my spirit rise up;
let the darknesses in us go down.

O God shield my heart from distress;
give protection from evil and wrong.

And O God bless my body
To be close to my soul,
So I enter whole into life
With the dear Child of Mary.

From *Stations* by Simon Bailey

Contents

Acknowledgements

I would like to acknowledge the help, advice and encouragement I have had from the following, who have either been instrumental in starting me on the road which led to this book, or have been part of my support group, and have fed me or bullied and cajoled me into getting on with writing it: Michael Metcalf (formerly Lichfield Diocesan Director of Education), Diane Lamb (formerly Children's Adviser, Lichfield Diocese), Lou Scott-Joynt, Kay Ansell, Jill Warren, Graham Fowell, Dan Tyndal, Stuart Petty, Angela Webb, Celia Harrison. I would also like to thank Hamish Bruce of Church House Publishing who has advised, encouraged and guided me through the production of the book. I hope they will not be disappointed with the end product and I thank God for all they have done for me and pray his continued blessings upon them.

Copyright Acknowledgements

I am grateful to the following for permission to reproduce material in this book:

Rosemary Bailey, extracts from *Stations* by the late Simon Bailey, published by Cairns Publications, 1991; Chris Beatson for the grace cube diagram; Kingsway Communications Ltd for A Parent's Creed; Kevin Mayhew/Palm Tree Press for Kitchen Prayer, Morning Prayer, Prayer for Serenity and Children Learn What They Live; The Reader's Digest Association Ltd, *The Gardening Year*, 1982, for the descriptions in Chapter 7; SPCK for A House Blessing, from David Adam, *The Edge of Glory*, SPCK, 1985, used by permission of the publishers; Tim Tiley for the prayer from Tours Cathedral, St Patrick's Breastplate, A Kitchen Prayer and On Children; Wild Goose Publications for the prayer on page xiv.

A House Blessing

God bless this house
from roof to floor
God bless the windows
and the door
God bless us all for evermore
God bless the house with fire and light
God bless each room
with thy might
God with thy hand
keep us right
God be with us
in this dwelling site

David Adam, *The Edge of Glory*

Introduction

Israel, remember this! The Lord – and the Lord alone – is our God. Love the Lord your God with all your heart, with all your soul, and with all your strength. Never forget these commands that I am giving you today. Teach them to your children. Repeat them when you are at home and when you are away, when you are resting and when you are working. Tie them on your arms and wear them on your foreheads as a reminder. Write them on the door posts of your houses and on your gates.

Deuteronomy 6. 4–9

T he picture of nurture which these verses paint is not that of a 'school', or even of a time set apart for religious instruction. Rather, it is one of an integrated everyday life which is coloured with conversations and symbols to remind each member of the family of the Great Commandment. The decorations in the house, the ornaments worn by individual members, and the family talk all carry reminders of God's presence. Nurture is continual and takes place at the same time as the ordinary activities of everyday life which have all been marked in some way by reverence for God and remembrance of his teachings.

That is what this book is all about – bringing God into the everyday life of your family, the things you do already, like taking the children to school, cooking meals, watching TV, getting up in the morning, having a day out or pottering in the garden. Family life today is so hectic. Probably both parents work and the children have numerous after-school and weekend activities, so it is difficult to put aside a time to give to God, on your own or with the family. Anyway, God does not want just a short bit of your time, even every day – he wants all your time, he wants to be an integral part of your life and your family's life, all day and every day.

Practising your faith at home needs to be rooted in something you already do. You must ask yourself how we can bring God into what we do as a natural part of our family life. There is, of course, a place for special times with God, when we concentrate specially on our relationship with him, and for special activities with your family, not least when we join with other children of God at church for worship. But I would like to encourage you in this little book to try some ways of making God that integral part of your life in everyday activities.

This is not a book to sit down and read from beginning to end (although you can do so if you wish) but it is a book to dip into and try things out. Not everything will work for you; your life style is unique to you and it is not for me or anyone else to prescribe what you should do, so do not feel guilty if you try something and it does not work. Leave it a while and try something else, think about why it did not work and that may help you to choose something else to do. Some of the ideas are more appropriate for Mum or Dad, some relate to small children, some to teenagers. Chapters on the car or the garden will not be of any use to you if you don't have a car or garden; if you live in a tiny flat or a large house different things will be possible for you. The size of your family, the age range of the children, will all affect what is useful to you and what isn't. My hope is that there is something for everyone, and even if the ideas in the book don't suit you they will encourage you to think of how you can best live out your faith in the home with your family. The ideas are only suggestions and you may be able to think of much better ones than mine.

The book is arranged in chapters which relate to different rooms in the house, plus the garden, the car and holidays, as well as general chapters on celebrating special events, festivals, milestones, and sad times. You may find it useful to look at the relevant chapter when you come to redecorate a room, which is a good time for innovation and changing things around; or when you buy a new car (I love buying and sticking on car stickers when we have a 'new-second-hand' car), or prepare for your holiday – but you do not have to wait that long. The index will guide you to different themes within the chapters.

The suggestions are intended to keep in mind the love of God for each member of the family as they bustle round the house, but they also should stimulate conversation about things that happen, or things that we are doing. This book should create opportunities for talking about the stories and the faith we hold and the whys and wherefores which crop up in daily living, and so enhance the personal relationships within the family. It is about helping you in your spiritual journey and how to make that real in the home with your family. You need to be able to do these things comfortably without feeling burdened. The important thing is to try to give you some ideas that you can use at home. These might help you to make your faith real within the home as well as being real when you are actually in church worshipping, and might be a sign for you and other people that come to your home, that yes, *God is Here*!

Both adults and children spend so little time at church or in church groups nowadays that our faith is not given much chance to blossom. It is essential that we spend time at home nurturing that faith and carrying it into our ordinary lives. I hope this book will help you and your family to do that and that you will all grow into the maturity of Christ Jesus.

> *Almighty God, Who has set us in families so that we may understand Your fatherhood in the great family of the Church; we pray for all who seek to make a place for You at the hearths of home. Open Your word again in the houses of our people, inspire parents to lead and to teach the young in prayer, that the daily worship of our land may ascend from every Christian home, and Your sufficiency be known again in things both great and small. Amen*

From *The Whole Earth Shall Cry Glory*
Revd George F. Macleod

1

The kitchen

Go into the place where you cook, the kitchen.

Stand by the cooker, the fridge,
or the washing machine.
Perhaps put the kettle on ...
Life goes on here too, but in a different way –
preparation, cleaning up, work,
washing, ironing, storing,
and, again, talking, thinking, planning –
a busy place for many people,
an easy place to wait and pray,
while hands are busy with other things.

Say:
Living God,
living and strong,
loving and gentle,
pour mercy upon us.

Think about these words:
O God shield my heart from guilt;
fill our bodies and spirits with joy.

Pray for
all who work here and the care they take;
the arrogant and proud who never serve
and are afraid to care.

From *Stations* by Simon Bailey

For me the kitchen has always been the hub of family life. It is where we eat, drink coffee with our friends, it's always warm and cosy, and it always seems to be the place where we have a 'talk'. Whatever your kitchen is like, see if a few of these ideas fit into it.

Preparing meals

It is good to share in the preparation of meals. It is good to share in any job around the house, but preparing a meal and eating together have always been an important ritual in bonding people together and celebrating. This is so evident in the Eucharist, 'We are one body because we share in one bread.' Often today families rarely eat together because they are coming and going at different times, and meals are often grabbed in haste from the fridge or microwave.

It is important to try to make one time in the week when you can all be together at a meal, sharing the preparation and the eating, making it a special occasion, putting candles on the table and some flowers and saying a prayer of thanksgiving before the meal, and maybe having time for talk after it as you all sit round the table. Even do the dishes together! It could be the start of an evening together when you can watch an appropriate video, or play board games or other games together – try Bible Trivia! There is more on this in Chapter 3.

Charity box

You may already have a charity box, perhaps, like me, one from the Children's Society. Giving to others less fortunate than ourselves is one way of giving thanks to God for all his blessings to us, and show-ing our care for his children who need our help. At the end of the week I put all my copper coins into the box. It doesn't seem much but over a year it mounts up to quite a lot. I hate those fiddly five pence pieces so I have another pot for them, so that when Christian Aid Week envelopes arrive or some other good cause I want to contribute to, then they get whatever is in that pot at the time.

- Or how about a Sunshine Bag/Pot? Every day the sun shines put a coin in the bag, then periodically empty the bag and send to your favourite charity. This is a good way to encourage the children to give a little of their pocket money.

- Or perhaps you could have a 'Thank you pot' to put something in whenever there is something you specially want to thank God for. I'm sure you could think of lots of things to thank God for – your health, your family, your job, the birds and flowers in your garden, all the blessings he showers on you.

Prayer board

The kitchen might be a good place to put up a prayer board – just the usual piece of cork board with a pencil and some bits of paper and drawing pins. Everyone puts up a note of something they would like praying about and every time you pass the board you can say a silent prayer when reading one or more of the notes. The notes need to be removed as situations change – some will stay up for a long time, others just for a day. The person who wrote the note should be the one to take it down. My family have taken to sticking sticky Post-it notes on a particular part of the kitchen wall, and these are very quick and easy to stick up, don't leave marks and are easily removed. Or you could use a white board and pen which can easily be rubbed off. Don't forget to put the board at a height that everyone can reach! You might like to put a line of verse across the top: 'O Lord, hear our prayers' or 'Lord, you know our needs before we ask'. You might like to have a special time each week when you come together and talk about the various requests and you could all pray all of them as a family. You could even suggest a similar board in church for the church family to use and include in intercessions.

- How about putting up an old Christmas card or Easter card each week and praying that week for the person who sent the card?

- A birthday/anniversary list would help you to remember to send a card and to pray for that person all week.

A Kitchen Prayer

Bless all this little kitchen, Lord,
including every nook,
And bless me as I clean the sink,
scrub pots and pans, and cook.

May every meal that I produce
be seasoned from above
With Tender Loving Care, of course,
But most of all Your love.

So bless this little kitchen, Lord,
and all within its care.
May they find warmth and cheer
herein as well as tasty fare.

© Tim Tiley

Kitchen Prayer

Lord of pots and pans and things,
since I've not time to be
a saint by doing lovely things,
or watching late with thee,
or dreaming in the dawn light,
or storming heaven's gates,
make me a saint by getting meals
and washing up the plates.

Although I must have Martha's hands,
I have a Mary mind,
and when I black the boots and
shoes, thy sandals, Lord, I find.
I think of how they trod the earth,
each time I scrub the floor;
accept this meditation, Lord,
I haven't time for more.

Prayer cards

I like to use prayer cards (as you will gather as you go through the book), similar to the ones produced by Tim Tiley Prints and Palm Tree Press. They have each published a Kitchen Prayer, but you can write your own in your own words on a piece of card. Mine might read 'Lord, you know what a rush I am in as I cook this meal, help me to concentrate on what I'm doing so that the family gets a feast blessed by you and not a burnt offering.' Stick it up where you will have opportunity to read it – perhaps over the cooker where you may be standing mixing sauces, or doing a stir fry, or over the sink to read when washing up. If you are lucky enough to have a dishwasher, how about a prayer of thanks on the door!

Many routine jobs, like washing up or ironing do not, as one person put it to me, 'occupy much of me', so the unoccupied bit can be praying. Remember, prayer is a conversation with God. You can share with him whatever is on your mind or heart and give him space to respond and talk to you. Be honest with God; he knows what is on your heart and mind so you cannot kid him about your feelings. It's better to bring them into the open and if they are not very nice feelings, ask God to help you to change them.

Tea towels

You can also buy tea towels with prayers or passages of Scripture on them. Hang them on the wall, as both decoration and reading matter. You could even use them for drying the dishes and read the inscription before you hang it up when the job is done. I bet everyone who helps to dry up will read it at some point too!

The inscription does not have to be overtly Christian; a friend gave me a pot holder inscribed with 'Anne's Kitchen – Happy is the home that welcomes a friend'. Perhaps this might be more meaningful to non-Christian friends who visit you?

Posters

There are some good posters available today; some have a line of Scripture, a message, a prayer, a meditation, or cartoons which set you thinking. They will appeal to some people, but not to everyone. If you have time, you might like to make your own posters with the children, portraying thoughts that are uppermost in the family at that time and find an appropriate verse of Scripture or prayer, or your own thoughts, to put on it. It is a good idea to change the posters before they get tatty and lose their impact!

Plants and flowers in the kitchen

Fresh flowers and plants always cheer up a room and they can be put in the kitchen as easily as anywhere else, just to portray the beauty of God's creation.

- The **African violet** may move you to say a short prayer for the people in Africa who need our prayers, or even to put a few pennies in the charity box (see p. 2). Its species name is *Saintpaulia*.

- **Busy Lizzie** might make you think of Martha and Mary, or a friend or relative called Lizzie.

- The **Peace Lily** might suggest a prayer for peace at home or abroad or for yourself and your family: 'Lord give me that peace which the world cannot give.'

- The **spider plant** might suggest a prayer or a parable about children and young people drawing strength from their parents and Christian community until they find their own place to root and grow independently in their own strength; or the strength of the community being drawn from God; or even a prayer for our own strengthening by being firmly attached to God and needing no other sustenance.

- **Ferns** are good to grow in dark corners as long as you keep them well watered. A collection of different varieties can make a green oasis, very soothing and calming.

- The **parlour palm** or **cast iron plant** will stand bad light, gas fumes, extremes of temperature and neglect, so it is good for those without green fingers!

- **Cyclamen** are always popular and come in a lovely range of colours. Put one in the middle of your ferns for a splash of colour.

- **Poinsettia** is always available at Christmas and now comes in colours other than bright red.

- **Ivies** are easy to grow, as is the **cheese plant** and **tradescantia** – **Wandering Jew** – and of course the **Christmas cactus.**

Children's pictures

Children at pre-school groups and early primary school bring home their pictures and things they have made and often the kitchen is the best place to stick these up either on a cork board or with magnets on the fridge, or blu-tack on the wall. It is important to praise these early efforts, and they present an opportunity to say something about God. 'He made the beautiful world you have put into the picture'. 'You are a creator like God'. 'God loves you and so he loves your picture too'.

Calendar

Our calendar is always hung in the kitchen by the phone so things can be booked in easily and dates checked. Your Christian bookshop will have some calendars with appropriate pictures and scriptural messages, but an attractive calendar showing the beauty of God's creation in a wide variety of ways is just as useful. You might like to add a 'thought' to the picture as you turn it over each month. Look for a calendar which has the Christian festivals marked on it.

Tim Tiley produce some little note pads with comments on – mine is in the shape of a hippo and the sentence is 'God made our beautiful world'. These are useful by the phone.

Mundane things

There are a number of mundane things to be done in the kitchen like washing up, ironing, mopping the floor, and as a friend of mine said, 'These jobs don't take up all my mind!'. So when doing these things the 'unused portion' of your mind is free to open itself to God. Let your thoughts wander through all the things that are 'on your mind', offering them to God and listening for his response. These can be valuable times of quiet with God if the family is not around, and often in the quiet the solutions to problems will strike us, or we remember things or people to pray for. You could write a prayer for the sink and the ironing board. 'Lord as I wash these dishes I give thanks that you provided the food that made them dirty, wash me also from my sins and keep me clean and sparkling for you'. As you iron the clothes you can pray for each person and thank God for the members of your family.

St Patrick's Breastplate

Christ be with me,
Christ within me,
Christ behind me,
Christ before me,
Christ beside me,
Christ to win me,
Christ to comfort and restore me,
Christ beneath me,
Christ above me,
Christ in quiet,
Christ in danger;
Christ in hearts of
all that love me,
CHRIST in mouth of
friend and stranger.

© Tim Tiley

2

The living room

Go into the main living area, the living room.

Sit down.
This is the base of your life.
This is where you live out your human existence,
living and crying, listening and singing,
talking, thinking, arguing, planning ...

Say:
Living God,
living and strong,
loving and gentle,
pour mercy upon us.

Think about these words:
O God bless the words that I speak;
give blessing to silence and talk.

Pray for those who share your life;
the lonely.

From *Stations* by Simon Bailey

J ust sit and look round your living room. Perhaps it is beautifully furnished and very tidy, perhaps there is a TV in the corner, wall units with favourite bits and pieces on them, some flowers and plants dotted around. If it is like mine was when the children were at home it will be chaotic, strewn with their bits and pieces, books, toys, craft work in various stages of production, newspapers and magazines.

Whatever it is like, there is an abundance of things in there which can remind us of God's goodness to us. The beauty of the flowers, plants, ornaments, all remind us of the joy of all that he has created. We can give thanks for our family as we trip over the roller-skates that we hunted high, low and level for last night and couldn't find, and as we tidy up behind the kids and our spouse. We can give thanks for how well off we are in comparison to most of the population of the world who have so little, and we can add a prayer for them and put something in the charity box.

Photographs

The living room is where you may have family photographs, but do keep them up to date as teenagers hate to have their baby photos on display when their friends call! Photographs bring to mind friends and family both near and far, so you can ask for a blessing on them or they could be a way of starting conversations about members of the family, especially those who have died. Say a little prayer for each one as you dust them.

Polished prayers

Dusting is a good time to pray. As you go round with the polish and duster remember the people who made the items of furniture, thank God for the beauty of the wood or china, remember the person who gave it to you and ask God's blessing on them. Some objects may lead you to think of other things, perhaps social or environmental issues – is your polish environmentally friendly?! Where did the furniture or object come from? Was it from a poor part of the world? You can pray for those people. You might even stick a piece of paper on the polish tin to remind you of things to think about while you work. If you are using a piece of 're-cycled' clothing or linen to polish with, you could write a message on it in felt tip or fabric paint – 'God polishes my house with love', and you can pray for the person who used to wear your duster. This almost makes you want to go and do the dusting to see if it works!

Cleaning the windows may make you think of the light they let into the house, and the light of Christ in your life and your home, or thoughts of seeing 'through a glass darkly'. Let your thoughts be a prayer.

The television

The TV takes a lot of flack these days about killing off conversation, about bringing scenes of sex and violence into the home for children to see and imitate. It can also cause a lot of family arguments over who is watching what and when. I must admit there are some programmes for both children's and adult viewing which I would not watch. On the other hand, because of TV we are now more aware of the plight of people all over the world and so are moved to help them. We know more about wildlife, both native to this country and other countries of the world, and the threat of extinction of so many species, for a variety of reasons. There is some good entertainment, music, drama, comedy, which we can enjoy together.

At the beginning of 1994, which was The Year of the Family, there were some very good programmes about the family. One described what happened when the TV was removed. Instead of the family spending time talking to each other, or playing board games, or doing crafts, the family actually spent less time together and less time communicating. The family gathered together to watch the TV and talked to each other about what they saw. Once the TV was removed, they all went their own way to do their own thing, homework in the bedroom or reading quietly on their own, etc. The television, like all modern inventions, has its benefits and disadvantages; it needs to be used wisely and controlled carefully and sensitively. Parents need to be aware of what the children are watching and to discuss with them why some things are not appropriate. And do not say 'because you are too young', which is no reason at all, but put it in other terms, and perhaps Christian terms: 'Would you still want to watch it if Jesus was baby-sitting with you?', 'Do you think he would enjoy it?', ' What do you think he would not like about it?'

One real benefit of the TV is the addition of a video recorder on which you can play family films for all the family to watch. There are good Christian videos available now, so how about suggesting that your church invest in some to set up a video library for all the families in the church to hire them – they are not likely to be found in your local video store! Or you could join together with a few other families and buy a few each and share them round, perhaps on the same basis as a baby-sitting circle where you gain points for lending and give up points for borrowing. Scripture Press produce a very good range of videos for all ages:

- Under fives: *The Toddler's Bible Video; Christopher Churchmouse;*

- Ages 5–7: *Quigleys Village;*

- Ages 5–12: *The New Adventures of McGee and Me;*

- Ages 5–13: *Secret Adventures;*

- Family viewing: *The Pilgrims Progress; The Chronicles of Narnia; Treasures of the Snow.*

They also produce some good teenage videos. See the Resource list at the end of the book for the Scripture Press address and other suppliers.

Again, the videos don't have to be overtly Christian. *The Chronicles of Narnia* can be enjoyed and the Christian messages come through; liken the death of Aslan to Christ's sacrifice, for example. You might enjoy *Jesus Christ Superstar* and *Joseph's Technicolour Dreamcoat* which tell the story in an offbeat way. *The Robe, King of Kings,* and *The Greatest Story Ever Told* are all in the video department of your high street stationers.

As the TV does tend to be the focal point of the sitting room, why not put some Christian artefacts on it – a small cross, or a prayer card, some dried flowers (not real ones as water should not be too near to electricity), just a reminder to thank God for your leisure and ability to watch TV and that he is Lord of what you watch. But remember that this is everyone's room and only do it if everyone is agreed, or can at least live with it, even if they don't believe.

Be careful not to impose things on your family, especially if they do not share your commitment to the Lord. This is particularly important if your spouse is not committed – the last thing you want to do is put people's backs up. Always negotiate! If you discuss what you want to do beforehand, usually the family will humour you if nothing else! I caused a near riot when, after redecorating the sitting room, I put up an icon instead of the usual pictures over the fireplace! The cross on the TV did not go down too well either!

Some children today are lucky enough to have a TV or computer in their room (see Chapter 5, The bedrooms).

Music

The living room may also be where you listen to music – perhaps you put it on while you do the housework or while relaxing. There is such a wide variety of Christian music on tape and records today, it is a pity to miss out on it. Your local Christian bookshop is bound to have a selection, from Cliff Richard to Cathedral Choirs, from Mission Praise to guitar instrumentals, from kids stuff to classical, Christian rock music to sung evensong. Talk to the assistants and tell them what sort of music you like and they will advise you. As the tapes are not cheap, again you might like to swop with other people or start a library of tapes at church. It is a great way of learning about new music to use at church and to share some joyful music with the family – soon you'll all be singing them (see Chapter 6, The garage and the car.).

Icons and pictures

Depending on the decor and design of your living room you can also use posters there, since you can get hangers for them or put them in glass frames. What message do you receive from the pictures on your wall? Think about it. Icons are beautiful, and they are sometimes called 'windows into heaven'. Pictures have always been and still are important ways of teaching the faith. Mosaics, carvings, wall paintings, stained glass windows and books have all been used in this way.

Icons are more than just religious pictures: they are a way of telling people about some complicated Christian teaching in a simple form that anyone can see and begin to understand. The people in icons are a little strange, and don't look like real people. At the end of time, we will rise to a new life in Christ, and then we will not look the same. Icons are meant to carry our prayers to Christ and the saints, because the people depicted in the icons are alive in heaven. The perspective in icons is unusual too. This is due to the window into heaven focus: you see through the icon into a scene that widens out for ever. In an Orthodox home there will be an icon corner which is a symbol that Christ is the centre of the home and it will be the place for family prayers and worship. I have one depicting Christ sitting on Mary's knee. Jesus looks like a miniature man rather than a baby to show that he was God even as a tiny baby.

You can buy icons in all shapes and sizes today so you can put them in any room of the house, but perhaps most importantly in the quiet area (see page 20) or wherever you say your prayers. Remember though that icons are venerated in the Orthodox Church and treat them with care out of respect for the Orthodox believers.

Christ the Light

Candles symbolise Christ as the light of the world. Most of us only use candles when the electricity supply is off, but why not have candles and light them, bringing the light of Christ into your home? Scented candles are great as they appeal to both sight and smell. Tim Tiley produces a card of the prayer used in Brecon Cathedral and in Tours Cathedral about lighting candles.

Also appealing to the sense of smell are the little oil burners which are so popular at present. The heat from the lighted candle underneath releases the aroma of the oil above. This can symbolise the light of Christ releasing the pleasant things in us, the vapour rising to heaven carrying our prayers thither, etc.

Lord, this candle that I have lit,
May it be LIGHT from you
to lighten my way
Through difficulties
and decisions

May it be FIRE from you
to burn up my selfishness,
my pride and all that
is impure within me.

May it be FLAME from you
to warm my heart
And teach me love.

Lord, I cannot stay long
in Your house,
This candle is
a little bit of myself
that I offer to you.
Help me to continue my prayer
in all that I do this day.

From a prayer used in the Cathedral of Tours

Quiet area

The living room may be the place in the house to have a quiet area. Everyone needs a time of quiet sometime and in a busy household this can be hard to find. A chair might be set aside in one room perhaps turned towards the window so that you can see out (if the view is attractive and peaceful) and you have your back to anyone who comes in (indicating 'I am having a quiet time, please do not disturb'); a table or ledge nearby might have a cross and candle, or prayer card or rosary or worry beads – things you can pick up and hold, like a smooth piece of wood or stone.

Sometimes use of the quiet area may indicate that someone has something on their mind and needs to confide. Be sensitive, you know your own family. Avoid intruding on the quiet area if you can and try to find a time for talking later. Be careful not to associate the quiet area with 'mother having a little chat to see if I'm all right' or no-one will feel inclined to use it. There is more on the quiet area in later chapters.

Books

The living room may be the room where you keep your books. Your local Christian bookshop will have a wide variety of books on all aspects of the faith so make time on your next shopping expedition to go in and browse. Most of the bookshops will give advice and help on setting up a bookstall in church (see Chapter 10, The church can help).

The range of children's books is wonderful today, and most of the Bible stories are available in simple versions for the young reader or for you to read to children. Ladybird and Lion books for children are perhaps the most attractive. Bibles now come in a multitude of versions: there is the *Toddler's Bible*, the *Beginner's Bible*, a cartoon version, the *Chronological Bible*, the *Dramatised Bible*, the *Good News Bible*, study bibles, and so on. It is no longer a case of buying one Bible that will last a lifetime, but buying appropriate versions for the age, ability and understanding of the person involved, thus making Bible reading accessible to everyone of every age. There are also Bible reading aids such as *First Light* from The Bible Reading Fellowship, and the *King*

Street series from Scripture Union (see the Resource list at the end of the book for the addresses of these publishers).

Reading the Bible should be a fun activity, not just another chore like homework. Mix Bible stories with other favourite stories at bedtime for the little ones. Use Bible story books as an enjoyable read for the early reader, and use the *King Street* series as a fun activity when you have time together or when children need something to do. When they get older there are some exciting adventure stories in a Christian context produced by Kingsway, and when it comes to the serious questions a study Bible will be helpful. For regular Bible reading The Bible Reading Fellowship produce Bible reading material for all ages.

I stumbled across a lovely children's magazine in my local newsagents called *Bible Stories*, which is suitable for early readers. It included the story of Noah's Ark, some activities on the story, pictures to colour and patterns to copy, animal chains to hang up, etc. This was followed by the story of the Good Samaritan together with an activity, and finally there was a prayer. It is produced by Redan Co. Ltd. (see the Resource list at the end of the book).

Hospitality

If you go into the homes of people belonging to eastern cultures you are overwhelmed with hospitality related to giving gifts to God in giving them to you; sugared almonds are associated with this and are always offered to visitors. Why not have a bowl of these little delights in the living room ready to offer to visitors? Remind the family they are for this purpose and not for snacks! There are other ways of showing hospitality: as soon as a visitor arrives at our house, on goes the kettle to make tea or coffee. Think about how you welcome visitors, and make them feel as welcome in your home as you would want to be in theirs. Be ready also to explain why you have prayer cards, posters, crosses and icons and goodness knows what else dotted around the house. You don't have to give a lecture but let the person know in very simple terms that you are a Christian. If they want to know more, they will ask – maybe not this visit but maybe next time you meet.

3

The dining room

Go into the place where you eat, the dining room.

Sit down where you normally eat meals.
Meals are more than sustenance;
they are human celebration, feast and joy,
friendship and sharing,
welcome for strangers
and the bonding of friends.

Say:
Living God,
living and strong,
loving and gentle,
pour mercy upon us.

Think about these words:
O God bless the folk I live with;
give blessing to our livelihood.

Pray for
the chance to share more;
the hungry and the poor.

From *Stations* by Simon Bailey

The meal

I have to admit that we rarely use the dining room. It's only for special occasions when we have visitors and cannot all fit around the kitchen table. However, whether it is just the family or is a party, eating together is an important event. It is worth trying to have one meal a week when the whole family sits down together and shares a family meal. For my family it is Sunday lunch and everyone knows that you don't arrange to do anything which will prevent you being there at one o'clock.

Having the meal in the dining room, if you have one, and laying the table with special care – perhaps some flowers in the centre of the table or some candles to light at the start of the meal, a bottle of wine and so on – make it special. Even if you are a family which at present does sit down together most of the time, having one 'special' meal each week establishes a good principle for the time when the family starts to do their own things when they get older.

Sunday for us has always been special, but for you some other time might be more appropriate – a week night or Saturday depending on the activities of the members of the family. We have traditional Sunday lunch of meat and two vegetables, but you could let a member of the family have a turn each week at choosing their favourite meal, so that it is their special meal and they get most of the attention that week.

Prayer

The special meal may be a good time for praying together. If you use the prayer board, this might be a time to look at the prayers on the board and give thanks for and remove those that have been answered and pray together those that are still ongoing. It is a good time to catch up on everyone's news and commit that to prayer.

There is no right or wrong way of praying. It doesn't have to be at the beginning of the meal; it may be much better to have the meal as a time of coming together and talking, and then commit everything to prayer at the end of the meal when everyone is relaxed and well fed. Prayers don't have to be formal and in liturgical language either. God is our friend and we can talk to him just as we would talk to our other friends. It may not even be necessary to have a time of prayer – the whole meal and talk may be your prayer, especially if there are members of the family who are not committed and would find formal prayer difficult.

An alternative to the prayer board is a prayer book, put perhaps on the sideboard if people pass it regularly. The prayers are written in the book during the week and then the book of prayers can be read at the family meal.

You might like to say grace at the beginning or end of the family meal. Again, these can be very simple from 'Ta Pa' or even 'Heavenly Pa, Ta!' to 'Rub-a-dub-dub, thanks Lord for the grub', 'Lord bless this bunch as they munch their lunch' or 'God bless these sinners as they eat their dinners'. There are books of traditional and modern graces, some of which are listed in the Resource list, or better still make up your own!

Beware also of making the grace a penance for some misdemeanour: 'You were last to the table so you can say grace!' or 'You didn't do your chores this week so you can say grace!'; equally, don't make it a reward: 'You have been such a good girl today you can say grace'. Prayer is not a reward or a punishment; it is always a privilege to speak to God, especially on behalf of others, so it is an important activity even when the words are simple and fun.

Grace at the beginning of a meal can be a frustration, especially for small children who cannot understand why the important and serious business of eating must be delayed, so a prayer at the end of the meal might be appropriate.

● **Make a grace cube**

A grace cube is fun to make out of cardboard (see the pattern on page 90). Write a grace on each square and then make up the cube. Someone rolls the cube and says the grace that appears on top. Beware though, this can cause arguments over whose turn it is to roll the cube, and even the person who has rolled it can object because they don't like the grace that appears on top! Vanpoules sell a prayer dice, so ask your vicar if he has their catalogue. UNICEF promote the Jar of Grace each year; they provide a sticker to put on a jar to put a coin in at every meal. Write to both organisations for further information (see the Resource list at the end of the book).

- **Make prayer cards**

   Another idea for prayer is to make a set of cards (or buy appropriate ones) and each person at the table picks a card at random and says a prayer. Either read the one on the card or say a simple prayer related to what is on the card. If you have small children who cannot read the cards, pictures of flowers, animals or people would be best and the prayer would be something simple like 'Thank you God for the flowers'. For older children it might just be a prayer 'prompt', 'Give thanks for something' or 'Pray for someone who is ill' or 'Pray for a member of the family'.

   If you make your own prayer cards you will need pieces of card about 7x12 cm. Write out the words of a prayer (if you have a computer you can print them in an attractive font), or write out the prayer prompt, or stick on a picture. Then cover the cards with 'sticky backed plastic' so they can be wiped clean. Look for a little box that they will stand up in, or a small paper rack so that they can stay on the table and not get lost.

After the meal

If you have the time, after the meal is a good time to talk with older children. This need not necessarily be 'religious' talk, but it could be about anything:

- exchanging news of what has happened that week;

- telling the youngsters about something important to the family;

- talking about an event that has happened in the family or in the community;

- discussing events in the wider world;

- you might play games;

- or watch a video;

- go for a walk;

- visit grandparents or friends or relations.

There is an old saying, 'the family that prays together stays together'. I'm not sure that is quite true but certainly the family that makes time to do things together will develop and strengthen relationships, and that is good for the family in many different ways.

Prayer for Serenity

God grant me
the serenity to
accept the things
I cannot change,
courage to change
the things I can,
and wisdom
to know the difference.

Reinhold Niebuhr
© Kevin Mayhew

4

The hall, porch, stairs, bathroom and loo!

The Door

Going through the door –

Leave it open
and think about the threshold,
the edge between the world outside and home,
your place of security and belonging.
There may be tensions here,
but inside the door you belong.

Say:
Living God,
living and strong
loving and gentle
pour mercy upon us.

Think about these words:

O God bless the journeys I make;
give blessing to travel and rest.

Pray for
each one who comes and goes through your door;
those who sleep in doorways, shut out from a home.

From *Stations* by Simon Bailey

Some people live in bungalows – no stairs!; some people have large halls with a sweeping staircase; some have a small square by the front door with the stairs leading straight from it between two walls. In some houses the back door is the one most used and that may lead straight into the kitchen or into a passageway. This chapter is about using these small areas and the entrance to the house as part of our Christian living.

The door

Often when we go out we are in a hurry, and when we come in we are tired after a day's work at school, or the office, or wherever. Entering and leaving the house are significant times. We leave the house to go out into the world leaving behind the privacy and security of our own home. When we return we return thankfully to that privacy and security. What can we do to mark that daily event?

● Perhaps we could put a small stoop of water (a reminder of our baptism) by the door so that as we go out or in we dip a finger in the water and sign ourselves with the sign of the cross, asking God to be with us as we go out into the world or giving thanks for returning home.

● We might have a cross by the door which we simply touch as we go in and out, again with a silent simple prayer for God's presence with us, or of thanks for our home.

● There are things to look out for in your Christian bookshop: in wood you may find a cross or the sign of the fish or a carved plaque with a motto, a suitable poster, or verse to hang up. There are 'stained glass windows' which you stick on to plain glass or some are in frames and you hang them in front of a window. They come in a variety of pictures and symbols and can be seen from both sides of the door – if you have clear glass. (You can use these in any room of the house, of course.)

- What about something that says 'Welcome' to anyone who calls, from a welcome mat to a poster (bought or home-made) which has a welcome message on it. If you enjoy cross-stitch or embroidery, there are kits with Christian messages on them which might be appropriate – far removed from the Victorian texts which could be a bit daunting!

- It is not easy to make entrances and hallways look warm and welcoming, but warm or sunshine colours for a small entrance always look good, and plants and flowers and cheerful pictures or posters help. Mobiles are attractive too. I have seen pottery and wooden doves, or perhaps chime bars. You may find these in gift and craft shops rather than in Christian bookshops. Children love making these. Simply cut out the shapes and fasten them with different lengths of thread to a coat hanger, or buy a lampshade ring from a craft shop (or rescue one from an old lampshade) to hang them from.

One home I visit has a nice entrance hall full of plants as it is filled with light from large windows, but the striking thing is the large cross on the wall, and I mean large – about 2 feet tall! It makes a very powerful statement to everyone who enters. Why not be bold with your statements about God?

The Stairs

Go through to the stairs.

Sit at the top of the stairs or in a passage.
Like the door this is another in-between place,
a place for movement and connection.
Why else do so many people like sitting on the stairs
to think and be quiet?
Stairs — going up — hint at hope
reaching, effort, risk, aspiration.

Say:
Living God
living and strong,
loving and gentle,
pour mercy upon us.

Think about these words:
O God let my spirit rise up;
let the darknesses in us go down.

Pray for
all the hopes of your household;
time to watch and think and reach up;
the hopeless and defeated.

From *Stations* by Simon Bailey

The stairs

Isn't it amazing how many different ways there are of going up and down stairs, children crawling up and coming down on their bottom, the light feet of a teenager going out on a date, the slow tread of the elderly, or the tired? What can we put on the wall by the stairs? Probably not things to read as it could be dangerous to stand on the stairs reading and you probably wouldn't stop anyway. Symbols would be better things that just catch the eye – a picture of a dove in flight up the stairs with you, a mobile or chime bars. A poster or special picture on the wall facing the head of the stairs which you will see on your way up; a cross or a statue of a saint. Again, plants can be attractive in hanging pots over the stairs or cascading over the banister rail if you have one.

The landing at the top of the stairs can be very useful; if it is only small, just a narrow passage, there is plenty of wall space to hang pictures and posters. There might be enough room to put up a small shelf and make a small 'shrine' with a cross or statue, a candle and a prayer card. If you have a larger landing, this could be the place to make your quiet place with a comfy chair, and a table or shelf with various things on to give a focus for prayer. You might include 'worry beads', useful to play with when you first sit down to help you relax, a candle to light (and the matches, provided you don't have little fingers who would play with them), a Bible, perhaps, or a book of prayers, or a selection of prayer cards.

Go into the place where you wash, the bathroom.

Fill the sink.
Splash the water on your face ...
This is the place of refreshment and cleansing,
restoring freshness.
Like that first splash of cold water in the morning ...
Bathing and washing are full of echoes
of inner cleansing and renewal.

Say:
Living God,
living and strong,
loving and gentle,
pour mercy upon us.

Think about these words:
O God shield my heart from distress;
give protection from evil and wrong.

Pray for
a refreshed and renewed spirit
for all who use this room;
those who feel guilty and dirty,
stale and corrupt.

From *Stations* by Simon Bailey

The bathroom

The bathroom is probably not a place to linger, especially in the morning when everyone needs it to get ready to go out. So again, symbols are useful: the fish has to come into its own in the bathroom! You can buy fish-shaped soap and sponges, fish-shaped dishes to hold soap or pot pourri, fishes on the towels, and even a fish wallpaper border or tiles. I found a stone fish for the cord pull!

Plants, crosses, and pictures can also be used, but posters may not stand up to the steam. Prayer cards can be used, especially by the mirror which most people will use to a greater or lesser extent. Put a morning prayer or an evening prayer by the side of the mirror.

> 'Lord bless me this day as I go about my work.
> Let me never forget that wherever I am, you are there
> with me to guide and support me.'

> 'Lord thank you for this day and all that has happened
> and for the rest to come as I go to bed.'

> 'Lord, as I wash my outside with soap and water,
> I pray you will wash clean my heart and mind
> with your Spirit that I may be a temple
> fit for you to dwell in.'

> 'As I wash myself may I be made clean and pure within.'

> 'Cover me this day with the shadow of your wing,
> even as I cover my body with these clothes.'

If you enjoy embroidery, or you know someone who does, how about stitching a few words onto the towels? There is usually a woven strip near the end which could be used.

Traditionally the loo is a place for quiet contemplation and humour! Why not put up a selection of cartoons, both religious and secular to have a giggle at, or some funny postcards. In one loo I visited there was a Christian alphabet poster for the children to read. You might put some holiday photos up to remind you of the good time you had and the people you shared the holiday with. Or some short texts – you are supposed to have time to read them in here! Plants come in handy again if there is room: ferns and such like don't mind if there is not much light and they like the steamy atmosphere.

5

The bedrooms

Go into the place where you sleep, the bedroom.

Lie down on the bed ...
This is the place for sleep and rest,
for the ending of the day.
For many it is a place of love too.
For some it is a place of sickness.
It is a very personal place,
a place of dreams,
of long thought into the early hours,
of tears and pain,
private possessions and treasures.
With the thought of sleep
there is always the near or distant echo
of death and final rest.

Say:
Living God,
living and strong
loving and gentle
pour mercy upon us.

Think about these words:
O God bless my body
To be close to my soul,

So I enter whole into life
With the dear Child of Mary.

Pray for
rest, a quiet mind, a good death;
the bedridden, the restless, the loveless.

From *Stations* by Simon Bailey

Some things will be more appropriate for Mum and Dad, some things more appropriate for teenagers, particularly in the bedrooms, where the items that go into a teenager's room are very different from those in a small child's room. Whereas things in the living room are going to be what everyone can accept, the bedroom is very personal and each person must decorate and live in it in their own way.

The nursery

Babies are the easiest members of the family to work with as they can't object to what we put in their room and many of the things become treasured possessions which they will never part with as they get older. So when you are decorating and setting up the nursery, you can let your imagination run riot. Look for appropriate wallpaper – Noah's Ark was one I saw – or you could use stencils of all types and descriptions. Mobiles, of course, are very popular: make one out of symbols or characters from Bible stories. Palm Tree Press produce Bible cut-outs which you might use (see Resource list). A cross is a must, either free-standing or hung on the wall, preferably where it is very visible from the cot and to everyone who walks in. Statues are nice too, such as a Virgin and Child especially for the nursery, and of course pictures and posters go well in any room. Embroiderers could do a 'birth' sampler with baby's name, parents' names, date of birth, and a blessing.

Pray with and for your babies as often as you can, bless them and sign them with the sign of the cross and commit them to his safe-keeping. The Lord's Prayer is for all ages and should be said to and for the baby from the first day – soon enough they will be able to join in with you. It is good to know a few prayers by heart, as they stand us in good stead throughout our life, especially in those times when we can't find our own words to use because of great sorrow or great joy. My mother now has senile dementia and gets very confused but she can still say the Lord's Prayer perfectly! The evening collect is short and easy to say.

> *'Lighten our darkness, Lord we pray, and in your mercy defend us from all perils and dangers of this night; for the love of your only son, our Saviour Jesus Christ. Amen.'*

A Parent's Creed

I receive this little one
as a gift from Your hand.
I trust in Your wisdom
as I attempt to stand
for those things in life
that are just and true
that will one day help
this child find You.

When you pray with your baby it is a good time to establish a routine which can be adapted for older children. Remember ACTS:

Adoration

Confession

Thanksgiving

Supplication

which gives shape to our prayers.

Adoration can be quite short, and keep it simple for the little ones:

> *'We praise you Lord*
> *for your everlasting goodness to us'*

> *'We love you Lord, our Redeemer'.*

Confession is when we say we are sorry for doing something – both parent and child. Don't let prayer be one-sided; listen to your child saying his or her prayers, but also pray with him/her. Say you are sorry too and always claim God's forgiveness at the end. This could be something like:

> *'Lord you became a person like us so you know*
> *our failings, forgive us for all the things we*
> *have done today that we are sorry for, so we*
> *may sleep in peace and start afresh tomorrow.*
> *Amen.'*

Children need to know they are forgiven and as God cannot give them a hug, you can do it for him and assure the child of both your and God's everlasting love.

Thanksgiving is the place to thank God for the good things of the day – the walk in the park, the ice-cream, the sunshine, the fun. Be explicit even though the ideas are simple and end with a general thanksgiving, 'Lord we thank you for all the good things you give us'.

Supplication. Having put ourselves right with God and thanked him for all he has given us, we are then ready to ask him for the things we need for ourselves and other people. Again, be specific, pray for those things that are relevant to the child. God knows what is in our hearts, the things we really want; we cannot ignore them and pray for what we think we ought to pray for – our prayers must come from our heart and soul not just from our minds. So pray for 50 ice-creams tomorrow (God only gives what is good for us not enough to make us sick!), for a teacher to be kind, for sunshine for an outing. A child's prayer will be for simple things but will be from the heart!

I don't use books of prayers because they have come from someone else's heart, not our own, and we can spend ages looking for the right prayer for the occasion instead of simply saying what we feel. However, *The Lion Book of Children's Prayers* is always popular; it has some morning and evening prayers, and some blessings which you might like to copy out on to cards to use regularly. It also has a good subject index where you will find entries such as Birthdays, Family, Forgiveness, Holidays, Homes, and so on.

Prayers for all the Family by Michael Botting is another good book, with a section of family prayers including a monthly cycle of prayer, Prayers at Festivals, Family Prayers, Thanksgiving and Graces. A lovely bedtime book is A *Story*, A *Hug*, and A *Prayer* by Michael Forster.

If you have time, you could help your child to make some prayer cards or their own book of favourite prayers, choosing some from the books and writing some of their own.

Growing up

Once they can talk children will start to ask for things they want in their room. Guidance is as important here as it is in watching TV. We want to encourage little ones to surround themselves with cheerful positive images, not only religious but secular images that speak of love and care and the beauty of the world around us. These not only show God's love for us all but also encourage a good self-image in the child and a feeling of being surrounded with love and care. Time is the great problem here because we need to give time to children as they grow, time to say prayers with them, read stories to them, give them attention so that they know they are important to you and that we love them and God loves them. You will have to adapt your routine to their needs as they grow, so try to make quality time to spend with them. You never get these early years back and even though it is hard work looking after the family, enjoy this lovely age.

When they go to school their ideas will develop very quickly and they will be influenced by their teachers and their friends. Again, guidance is the key word; it is difficult for children to swim against the tide in a secular world, so guide and encourage and support their delicate and fragile faith in what you are and what you do. Buy and/or borrow from the library Christian story books and non-Christian books with interesting and positive stories in them. Encourage the children to pray their own prayers – you could use the prayer card idea from the Dining room chapter (see page 26). Use prayer prompts rather than prayers so they can pray in their own words.

You might like to have a space on the wall or on the cupboard doors covered with photographs of family and friends as a prompt for prayer – 'Who haven't we prayed for lately?', 'Grandad has a cold, let's pray for him tonight', and so on. Include those loved ones who have departed this life as it is important to name them and pray for them, even the dog and cat. Part of the grieving process is the need to remember them and still love them even though they are no longer with us and, especially important for children, that they are spoken about. A Morning Prayer card and Evening Prayer card by the bed could be used, so you say a simple prayer together when you get them up and put them to bed. Small children soon learn these by heart even when they can't read them and will remember them all their lives.

Remember that the prayers have to grow up as the child grows up if they are to be meaningful and not just a ritual at bedtime. There will come a time when the child will want to pray on their own, when their relationship with God has developed into a personal relationship and they want to talk to him in private. Probably there will be a time when they say their own private prayers after Mum or Dad has gone and they are alone. You will need to be sensitive to this and judge when is the right time to leave them to say their own prayers. It will probably tie in with other things like reading their own book at bedtime and putting themselves to bed, but you will need to continue to encourage them in their prayer life by your example and perhaps by looking for useful prayer books or Bible reading aids which include prayers. The Bible Reading Fellowship produces material for all different ages.

Teenagers' room

Teenagers will choose their own posters to adorn the walls, and their own treasures to scatter around. They will reflect their faith in their own way and the only influence we can or should have is in the way we reflect our faith in the home. They may want to copy us or be the opposite to us; either way, it is for them to do their own thing. Teenagers, especially the girls, tend to like things like joss sticks and perfumed candles when they are old enough to use them safely, as aids to prayer and meditation.

Teenagers get into pop culture and issues. They are likely to espouse causes such as homelessness, famine, or environmental issues. They are trying to make sense of the world around them and have a strong sense of justice. Their rooms are likely to be a seemingly odd mixture of pop stars, posters on issues, and Christian symbols; treasured things from their childhood alongside the latest teenage gear. It is a time for asking questions and seeking understanding. Parents need to encourage and support this stage rather than trying to give the young-ster all the answers. It can be a time of wonderful 'theological' discussions when our adult beliefs can be challenged to the limit, but we can grow in our faith as we talk to our children. Perhaps the most

Children Learn What They Live

If a child lives with criticism
he learns to condemn.
If a child lives with hostility
he learns to fight.
If a child lives with ridicule
he learns to be shy.
If a child lives with shame
he learns to feel guilty.
If a child lives with tolerance
he learns to be patient.
If a child lives with encouragement
he learns confidence.
If a child lives with praise
he learns to appreciate.
If a child lives with fairness
he learns justice.
If a child lives with security
he learns to have faith.
If a child lives with approval
he learns to like himself.
If a child lives with acceptance
and friendship he learns to find love in the world.

© Kevin Mayhew

important thing to do at this time is to keep the communication chan-
nels open and pray for our teenagers. Remember that God is seeking
them just as they are seeking God!

Many young people today have a TV or computer in their room and
spend most of their spare time in their own room 'playing' with the
computer or watching TV. This has two major implications for the family. First, it means that the family are not together as much as they
could be, and the ideology of individualism (every one doing their own
thing) is fostered. Second, it makes it much more difficult for parents
to monitor what the young person is watching and doing. We have to
be aware that not all TV programmes or computer games are the sort
of thing we would want our children to see. How you handle this situation depends very much on your relationship with the youngster but
the important thing is to talk to them and not let them cut themselves
off from the family by being isolated in their room.

Parents' room

The parents' bedroom may be open to the family at any time or may be
a very private room which the children rarely enter, and that may vary
with the age of the children. Anyway, it is your room and you do what
pleases you. Think about posters, pictures of the family, flowers,
crosses, icons. How about a prayer place in the quiet of your room, perhaps a table and chair by the window with your Bible reading and
prayer aids there? Or perhaps you read and pray in bed so that these
things are all on the bedside table or on the floor by the bed? Is this
the best room for a quiet area for all the family to use since the room
is unoccupied most of the family's waking hours? Is your spouse as
committed as you? If not, then think carefully about what you put in
the room as it is a special place for both of you!

Bedrooms are important places in the home whether they are shared
with siblings or spouses: they are personal places, places to retreat to
and be alone, places to be yourself, and so are good places for personal prayer. They are our own inner sanctum away from the world.

On Children

You may give them your love but not your thoughts,
For they have their own thoughts.
You may house their bodies but not their souls,
For their souls dwell in the house of tomorrow,
which you cannot visit, not even in your dreams.

You may strive to be like them,
but seek not to make them like you.
For life goes not backwards nor tarries with yesterday.
You are the bows from which your children as
living arrows are sent forth.
The archer sees the mark upon the path of the
infinite, and He bends you with His might
that His arrows may go swift and far.

Let your bending in the Archer's hand be for gladness;
For even as He loves the arrow that flies, so
He loves also the bow that is stable.

Kahlil Jibran
© Tim Tiley

Morning Prayer

Good morning, Lord.
Thank you for this brand new day.
Give me the wisdom
to see its possibilities,
the strength to face its challenges,
and the grace to be open to its promise.
Give me your heart of love to do a favour,
speak a kindness, offer a hand,
soothe a hurt, celebrate a joy,
share a sorrow, or in some small way
give of myself in love to another
in your name.

6

The garage and the car

Praying

Some of my best praying is done in the car when I am on long journeys on my own. At least there is no phone nor any people to interrupt my thoughts. Sometimes I put on a tape of Taizé or other music, but often I just drive in silence and let my thoughts surface and rise to God as they will. I think that is why we all need a quiet time with God, a time when our hearts and minds can open up to God. To begin with, the thoughts uppermost will be pretty business-like, but the longer we can rest in the Lord, then the deeper thoughts can rise. It is not so much a time for talking to God or asking him, but more of simply opening ourselves to our self and God. Perhaps, in fact almost certainly, when you are driving is not the best time in the world to do this but it just seems to happen when I drive, and I get little opportunity at home to be quiet and on my own.

One family I know took the opportunity of driving to school together to say prayers. One of the passengers read the prayers from a prayer card in the car. Again, this can be quite simple. Picture cards for little ones, simple prayers for the day for the readers, and prayer prompts for the older ones.

A super prayer tape is Angela Ashwin's *Patterns in Prayer* which is a series of meditations for busy people. Her books are also very good, especially *Patterns not Padlocks: Prayer for Parents of Young Children – and all those who Feel Frayed at the Edges, Stressed and Generally Pressurised, Squeezed and Harassed*!

There is also a motorist's prayer produced on a prayer card to keep in the car and say before you move off in the morning. It only takes a moment and you set off committed to God's care in a good frame of mind.

Music in the car

Many people have a tape deck in the car or even a CD player and enjoy music while they drive. There is a wide choice of tapes now. I have some 1960s tapes for me and Dad, guitar instrumentals of religious songs which the whole family enjoys listening to, Taizé and Iona music, traditional hymns for myself, and even a sung matins and evensong!

Take care in the choice of music; there are many very good artists and performers that are appropriate to the various age groups, from Captain Alan and his crew (a series of cassettes by a Church Army Children's worker) to American Christian Trash Bands. Whatever we encourage our youngsters to listen to, it needs to be very close to what they are listening to the rest of the time with their non-Christian friends, and it may help them to relate the Christian message to their non-Christian friends. Listen to their music even if you still have to ask them to turn it down! Watch *Top of the Pops*! Remember when you used to know the name of all the bands and try to stop yourself saying 'That's a load of rubbish', like your parents did. It doesn't have to be overtly Christian music: musicals like *Cats*, *Les Misérables*, *Joseph*, *Godspell* all have a Christian/moral message and are a jolly good listen! Try to go and see the show if you possibly can and the impact will be even greater! (see Chapter 8, Out and about!).

Church House Publishing produce a lovely book by Peter Churchill called *Feeling Good: Songs of Wonder and Worship for Five's and Under*. Many of the songs are to well-known tunes like Frère Jacques, Rock-a-bye baby and The wheels on the bus, but the words are Christian. The little ones will love these in the car or anywhere else, and will join in the simple but meaningful words.

Long journeys with the family can be quite traumatic with the kids wanting to know if you are there yet only ten minutes after you have left home. As part of the packing routine, in addition to the usual refreshments and tapes, fill a bag each with things like:

- colouring/worksheets (try Susan Sayer's book *Including Children* and/or ask at your local Christian bookshop or ask the children's work leader in church if they have any);

- scrap paper, pens, pencils, felt tips, etc.;

- books, some of a religious nature, some not!

- comics and magazines;

- leaflets about the place you are going to so you can plan and talk about it on the way there.

Play 'I spy church spire' and keep a tally of who spots a church tower or spire first. When they see one, they shout (not too loudly of course!) 'I spy church spire', and one person keeps a record, with a reward at the end of the trip for the one who spotted the most. This will be an on-and-off event as the journey progresses (or you could play 'I spy car stickers'; see below).

Car stickers

You can buy a wide range of Christian car stickers from a discreet fish symbol to a banner headline for the back window. A friend of mine has so many on her car that the boys won't borrow it any more, especially to go to football matches (another advantage if you have car-driving children)!! Seriously, this is a way of witnessing to your faith wherever your car goes, and can start up conversations with those who see them, and ensure friendly waves from fellow Christians who mark their cars in the same way.

The car has to be the ideal place to have a St Christopher, patron saint of travellers. You could hang it somewhere very visible or tuck it away secretly. How about leaving one hidden in the car when you change it, for the protection of whoever buys your car, and perhaps they will be influenced by the stickers and so on if they are left on?

And finally

As Christians, we must recognise our responsibility to be stewards of God's creation and we should therefore behave responsibly as car own-ers.

Protect the environment by:
Keeping your car properly serviced to reduce harmful emissions.
Using unleaded petrol if you can.
Not making unnecessary journeys; plan to do as much as possible in one journey instead of making three.

Protect people by:
Keeping the bodywork tidy so no one will injure themselves on it.
Driving carefully at all times and observing the speed limits.

You will find that this actually saves you money, time, hassle and speeding fines, whether your car is a battered old Mini or a new Rolls Royce!

The garage

Your car, like mine, may have to sit outside in all weathers, but if you have a garage you can put up some reminders in there. Perhaps you use it for more than just putting the car in, perhaps the freezer, and washing machine are in there or it is someone's hobby area.

Posters are probably your best bet. How about a poster of a really fabulous car but put on it the words 'Oh you'll never go to heaven in a ...!' Or put up in large letters which you can see through the windscreen a short prayer for going and coming.

> 'Lord let me drive safely and may we all
> be protected by You on our journey'.

> 'Thank you Lord for a safe journey and
> return home'

Over a hobby area, perhaps 'Lord of all creation, we are one in your continuing work'. Over the washing machine 'Thank you Lord for this machine and all that it does' or even 'You'll never go to heaven in a washing machine!' You could add a prayer for those who still have to wash clothes in a river and have never even heard of a washing machine or even clean running water on tap. Something similar could be placed over the freezer, praying for those who are starving. Perhaps a penny could also go in the charity box (see page 2)?

Crosses go well anywhere and are a discreet but meaningful symbol for everyone.

7

The garden, garden shed, greenhouse and conservatory

I n Genesis God created the man and the woman and told them to go forth and multiply and have dominion over all the Earth. This could be interpreted as sex and gardening or perhaps more accurately as Relationships and Stewardship. Relationships include our relationship with God, with our families, with our neighbours at home and abroad. Stewardship means caring for God's creation whether that is by using CFC-free aerosols, being careful with our car, recycling our waste or looking after our own garden, backyard, or window box.

Including plants with biblical names in your garden can be a source of witness to your friends, a reminder to yourself and a talking point with your children. For example, when friends ask the name of your lovely climber which is a Passion flower, you can explain why it is called that and what all the parts stand for (see p. 62). Or when your children are helping with the gardening, you can tell them the name of the plant – say Joseph's coat – and remind them of the story of Joseph's many-coloured coat and the problems he had with his brothers, etc.

If you have borders and bedding plants in your garden perhaps you could cut out a bed in the shape of a fish or a cross. This might encourage comment and conversation with neighbours and passers-by.

The front garden is your witness to the whole world. While the back garden is more for family and friends, both gardens can be powerful witnesses to your faith.

Here is a list of some plants to look out for:

- *Hermerocallis* - 'Gentle Shepherd'

  A Day Lily with a gentle pastel colour. Tell the lost sheep story.

- *Yucca Filamentosa* - 'Adam's Needle'

  Evergreen often classified as a shrub. It is a large plant reaching 6' high with a 5' spread. From mid to late summer it produces its magnificent white flowers. Adam and Eve story.

- *Helleborus Niger* - Christmas Rose

  Flowers throughout the darkest months of winter: height 12–18". Though evergreen the leaves tend to die back after flowering in the first year after planting. Plant it where it can be seen from the house or as you walk to the door. Mary is likened to a rose, but any Christmas story could be told, especially stories of hope and light.

- *Helleborus Orientalis* - Lenten Rose

  Slightly taller than the Christmas Rose and flowering Feb/March. Plant with the Christmas Rose.

- *Dicentra Spectabilis* - Bleeding Heart

  A popular graceful perennial plant. Many-arched sprays of heart-shaped red and pale pink flowers produced from April until June.

- *Aquilegia* - Monk's Head Lily

  Popular perennial, grows to 18" and flowers June–July

- Tulip 'Angelique'

  A bold, sturdy double-flowering tulip in pale pink. Height 18", flowers May.

• Daffodil 'St Patrick's Day'

Usually in full bloom on St Patrick's Day, 17 March. The novelty of this variety is that when the flower is fully out the cup becomes a lovely 'green' colour. There is also a gladioli called St Patrick's Day and one called Friendship.

• Anemones 'St Brigid'

St Brigid was a sixth-century nun who was renowned for her good works. The well-known flower which bears her name comes in a variety of colours, grows 10" tall and flowers April/June.

• *Ornithogalum Umbellatum* - Star of Bethlehem

A late spring flower which will grow in shade as well as sun. Masses of white star-shaped flowers, height 10", naturalises well.

• *Lilium Candidum* - Madonna Lily

Fragrant waxy white early flowering variety, height 3', flowers May/June. Mary's very well known symbol.

• *Polygonatum multiflorum* - Solomon's Seal

Dangling white bells on arching sprays in May/June, height 3', good for flower arranging. Stories of Solomon.

• *Polemonium* - Jacob's Ladder

The name comes from the double row of secondary leaves which are reminiscent of a ladder. Height 12" to 2' depending on variety, flowers May/June. Story of Jacob's dream.

- *Chamaecyparis Obtusa Nana Gracillis* - Temple Tree

  A slow low-growing conifer with a fascinating ornate shape with shell-shaped foliage of a dark green glossy nature. Ideal for a tub, height 4'.

- *Spiraea Shirobana* - Joseph's Coat

  Small shrub (3'), bearing both pink and white flowers, blooms June to October.

- Snowdrops also called Candlemas Bells, or Mary's tapers, flowering at Candlemas time (February), and signifying the purity of Mary.

- Asters - Michaelmas Daisy

  Although asters are commonly called Michaelmas Daisies the name only really applies to *Aster novi-belgii* which flowers in September/October. It makes a dense bush about 2'6" high on woody stems that usually do not require staking. They are easy to grow, hardy, herbaceous plants. There are numerous varieties, but look out for a pink called 'Fellowship', a blue called 'Moderator' (for the Presbyterian readers!) and a white called 'White Choristers'.

- *Passiflora* - Passion Flower

  Climber for a sheltered position, flowers June/September. How about making a large wooden cross to train the passion flower on? Two pieces of wood nailed together and perhaps some trellis fastened to it, leaving enough wood at the bottom to sink it into the ground in a border. This may be a very moving experience for you, bringing home the carrying and erecting of the cross at Easter. Or, if you are growing it on a wall, put up the trellis in a cross shape.

Each part of the flower has significance:

The five sepals and petals are the apostles less Peter, who denied Jesus, and Judas, who betrayed Jesus.

The three stigmas are the three nails.

The five stamens are the five wounds.

The corona is the crown of thorns.

And the five tendrils are the scourges.

- *Spiraea arguta* - Bridal Wreath

  Height and spread 6/8', dainty white flowers in April and May.

- *Cercis Siliquastrum* – Judas Tree

  Unfortunately grows to 25' with 20' spread but has lovely pea-like flowers in May before the leaves come.

- *Buddleia davidii* - Butterfly bush

  Can grow to 12' with a spread of 12'. It has purple spikes of flowers in graceful sprays in late summer. There are several named coloured forms. The joy of this shrub is that it is beloved of the butterflies, so you can enjoy a beautiful bush, watch the numerous varieties of butterflies and thank God for the beauty of his creation, and remember King David!

General

Look out for Bishop's bugs which have a pattern like a bishop's mitre on their backs – they like chrysanthemums and dahlias. You can add other plants to the garden with names that occasion a comment! Look out for *Aubretia* 'Mary Poppins', a little rockery plant; *Bergenia* – Bear's Ears because of the shape of the leaves; *Stachys lanata* – Lamb's ears or

Donkey's ears again because of the shape and furriness of the leaves, very tactile. Look out for varieties that are named after members of the family, or for an anniversary. These will all stimulate interest in the names of the plants in the garden and so help to develop conversations.

Be careful that you are not extolling the virtues of God's creation and then getting out a powerful insecticide to kill all the bugs he made! Weeds are his creation as well and often children like them better than your carefully cultivated varieties. You probably enjoyed making daisy chains as a child! Weeds are flowers growing in the wrong places and we can use environmentally friendly weed killers (they are usually safer for pets and children) to discourage them. Insects sometimes spoil our favourite plants and so need discouraging, but they are all part of God's creation – no aphids, no ladybirds! You might like to have a wild garden in a corner somewhere to encourage some of our threatened species like cowslips, primroses, poppies, etc. You can buy packets of wild flower seeds from any good nursery these days. Especially encourage plants that attract and sustain wildlife such as butterflies.

Window boxes and back yards

Even if you do not have a garden you could have a window box. It seems these are always filled with geraniums, allysum and lobelia, but look through the list above and see if there are any small plants you could put in your window box. A back yard (or front yard) can be made very attractive with large and small pots and tubs in which many of the plants above could be grown.

The garden shed

The garden shed is the butt of many a joke, and it may seriously be someone's bolt hole! Whoever the shed 'belongs to', it is up to them what goes in it, but there is no reason why amongst the garden tools and lawn mowers, compost and plant pots there shouldn't be some

reminders that we work with God in his continuing work of creation. A rough wooden cross, some posters, a verse ('And God saw what he had made and it was good', 'Some seed fell on good ground and produced 40, 60, and 100 fold') can be put up in the shed or even on the outside, and a cross can be put by the door to touch as you go in and out to remind you of God's work in creation and salvation.

The greenhouse and conservatory

The same applies to the greenhouse. You might put up two posters back-to-back on the same pane – one to be read from the outside and one from the inside. A cross or some stained glass put on the window would also be seen from both sides. You could also put a big cross on one of the windows in your conservatory, especially if it can be seen by passers-by.

Out and about!

To our forefathers, our faith was an experience.
To our fathers, our faith was an inheritance.
To us, our faith is a convenience.
To our children, our faith is a nuisance.

We all need time off occasionally and families need time off together to get away from home and work and school and all the demands of daily living. Try to make a habit of going out as a family regularly, whether it is a shopping trip (not the weekly groceries!), a visit to a theatre, social events at church, a day in the country or the seaside. Where you live and what resources you have will of course determine what you can do, but you might like to look out for or try some of the following.

Music and drama

Look out for adverts for concerts by Christian bands and groups. These are more likely to go to the bigger towns but even if you live in the depths of the countryside you may be able to get to one reasonably near to you. Your church can help in this (see below). There are also a number of Christian drama groups touring the country so watch out for these.

Going out to a concert, play, musical, etc. should be fun for all the family, so do not just stick to Christian things. Choose carefully from the secular activities in your area and go to the cinema, theatre, concerts, etc. that appeal to all the family.

Events

Days out can be spent at Christian and non-Christian events. Many dioceses have a big event for all the family every few years. Here in Lichfield we are having a big event at Stafford Showground in 1997 called 'The Feast' where there will be all sorts of activities for everyone from '0–90', ending in a big worship event. Look out for local church events for families and teenagers and children, encourage your church to put on parish picnics, day trips, and events. Our Deanery Links Scheme which networks all the Youth and Children's workers sometimes puts on a family outing when Mums, Dads and all the family can have a day out together – all organised for them. I met my best friend on a Deanery bus going to the Maundy Thursday Service at our Cathedral in Lichfield.

Wherever you live there are bound to be local beauty spots, working farm museums, historic houses and churches, theme parks which can provide you with a day out and time together. Perhaps you could join together with other families with children who are the same age as yours, especially if they have no transport and you do. It is usually possible to get reduced rates for parties to visit these places so you might organise a coach trip from church.

Retreats

In your diocese you may have a retreat house of some description where you could go for a weekend as a group of families. This is usually much cheaper than a hotel or boarding house and often they will put on a suitable programme for you. Lichfield is most fortunate in this as we have a residential youth centre in the Dovedale Valley which can cater for a group of families. The staff can provide excellent programmes for all ages and of course there are marvellous walks in that area. There are also retreat centres on the coast where you could stay for very reasonable rates, some are self-catering, some leave you to do your own thing, while others will put on a programme for you.

Most retreat centres put on activity retreats, such as painting or music retreats, and this could be an opportunity for you to get away from the family for a few days to immerse yourself in a favourite activity and, in and through it, to grow closer to God. Perhaps you enjoy painting – when you have time – so you might go on a painting retreat where there would be times of worship and prayer, perhaps discussion or talk about painting and lots of time to sit and paint. I like to go on a quiet guided retreat at the Loreto Centre in Llandudno, where for me the Welsh mountains meet the sea. I prefer self-catering so that I can eat all my favourite foods when I am hungry. Each day Sister Bridget spends an hour with me, giving me a Bible passage to meditate on, discussing the meditation of the previous day, and praying with me. The rest of the time I do what I feel like, as I think about the Bible passage, I walk on the beach, climb the Orme, sit by the sea, rest in my room, work on my tapestry. The first day I usually sleep a lot! I feel so much closer to God as I give him so much time, and listen to him. I always come back refreshed and reinvigorated but also much more peaceful, at peace with myself, God and everyone else.

We all need times of spiritual refreshment and time to grow into God and sometimes we need to get away from the family to do this. For information on retreats, look at a magazine called *The Vision*, published by the National Retreat Association, or look in your local Christian bookshop for an SPCK guide to retreats to find retreat centres in your area.

Holidays

Look out for Christian hotels, some privately owned, some owned by organisations such as the Methodists. These provide good accommodation at reasonable rates in a Christian atmosphere and again, some have programmes for you while others leave you to do your own thing. You will find adverts for these in your church newspaper such as *The Church Times*. Ask your vicar if he knows of any. You might be attracted to events like Spring Harvest, or Greenbelt which are week-long

Christian events for all ages. Again, your clergy person will know about these or look for adverts in church newspapers, or contact your diocesan office.

Holidays do not have to be Christian-based. A weekend at Centre Parcs will do much to refresh you and give you quality time with the family. Just as God wants to share our daily lives, he also wants to share in our holidays, wherever you go you take him with you.

The main family holiday is an important time of relaxation, a time for everyone to unwind and let their hair down. If you can afford it, make sure you get a holiday together as a family, but remember also that you and your spouse need time together without the children so try to get a weekend away, or even if you cannot afford to go away, a weekend without the children. When mine were little we could not afford holidays, but the children went for a week to their grandparents so that Richard and I had some quiet time at home without them and they had a change of scenery and activities. The section on the car may give you some ideas for things to take on the journey when going on holiday.

It seems to be the thing nowadays for children to 'sleep over' at their friends' houses and with a bit of organisation, you could arrange for your children to all be sleeping over at a friend's house for a weekend, and then you could return the compliment giving another couple a weekend of peace and quiet. Children need time away from their parents as well, so sleepovers benefit everyone, as long as you know the family they are staying with and it doesn't happen too often.

Can you make going to church as much of a fun outing as going to the park, or for a picnic? Why not try? This involves PREPARATION, SHARING and PRAYER (PSP). Do make preparations. I know it's a bit of a bore at the weekend, but if everyone knows you are going to church tomorrow and everything is organised the night before, like clothes to wear, the meat and vegetables prepared ready for lunch, or a picnic ready to take with you to go on to somewhere after church, it is less hassle on Sunday morning. Get up with plenty of time for everyone to get ready to go but with time to sit over an extra cuppa, and mooch round in a dressing gown for a bit so that it feels like a lazy day off! It also gives time for sharing. Within reason, let the children take favourite things with them to church if it helps them to feel comfortable and secure there. The main thing is not to be rushing round and getting wound up which makes the whole thing seem more trouble than it's worth and you will still be wound up all through the service and not be able to relax and worship. Hopefully your church will pick up or has already picked up many of the ideas in Chapter 10, because what happens when you get to church depends very much on the congregation and church leaders. You can perhaps encourage them to make being in church an enjoyable experience. Also encourage your friends and your children's friends to come with you, as it is always more fun if you have friends and family around you. Pray, yes, pray, about the service the night before, asking God to help you to relax and enjoy it, that the whole family will enjoy it and be strengthened and encouraged by it. If you feel it is right you might say a prayer before leaving the house to go to the service. Jesus wants us to enjoy being with him. I'm sure the disciples enjoyed his company and had many a laugh and joke with him, so let's enjoy his presence in the worship of the church.

9

Good times and bad times

All families have celebrations, important milestones to mark, and sad times of bereavement. These all need addressing and can be important times for acknowledging God's work in our lives, as well as times of testing of, and growing in, our faith.

Just think of all the milestones in our lives:

- birth
- baptism
- birthdays
- first word, first steps
- first day at playgroup/nursery
- new baby arrives in family
- first day at primary school
- moving up the classes
- first encounter with death – a pet or a person
- first day at secondary school
- first visit to hospital
- going to college
- first day at work – first pay cheque
- first date
- engagement
- marriage

- first baby
- subsequent babies
- changing jobs
- moving house
- first child leaves home
- last child leaves home
- retirement

Some of these events will happen every year and the way you celebrate them will become a family tradition, so be careful what you start, and don't forget what you did last year as it may well be expected again this year!

Birthdays

Birthdays are an obvious milestone and are important to everyone even when they are so old they ought to ignore them! Birthdays should be special days, when the person is the centre of attention and feels very special to their family and friends, but for some they may be a disappointment. Most years the birthday will fall on a busy week day so involve the person in the planning so that they know what to expect, but you can also plan a little surprise so that they get a bit more than they expected. Let the person choose a special meal, and decide who should be at the meal. The birthday cake is important; lighting and blowing out the candles can be a small ritual of counting and cheering/clapping and singing 'Happy Birthday'. When you light the candles you might like to sing 'Jesus bids us shine with a pure clear light'.

Photographs are an important record of special days. You might have an album just for birthday photographs and each year you can look through it and remember previous birthdays and the people who celebrated with you. Perhaps the birthday cards could be put in the album as well, or in a separate scrapbook and at bedtime prayers could include all the people who sent cards and/or came to the party. I keep

the cards up for about a month in the front room or they can be put up in the bedroom for as long as it suits you. When this year's photographs come back from the chemist you will need to make time together to put them in the album. Write the date on the back of the photograph.

You can buy lovely books now to record the early years and milestones of your child, first steps, first words, size, weight, colour of hair and eyes, special presents etc. Choose carefully and look for ones which record the baptism details.

Baptism

Baptism is an important event in the life of the child, its family and the church family. The day will be a time of celebration, a gathering of family and friends, a shared meal. Involve all the family in planning and preparing for the day, take lots of photographs on the day, including the clergy person who conducted the baptism (usually you can take photographs round the font after the service) and add a few of the interior of the church and the outside since you may move from that area and it may not be the church that the child grows up in!

Celebrate the anniversary of the baptism, lighting the baptism candle, looking at the photographs, perhaps inviting the godparents to share a meal with you, either on the day or on the nearest Sunday. You could all go to church together that Sunday and let the vicar know in advance why you will all be there so he can add something appropriate in the prayers.

Confirmation

The next step at church will probably be confirmation, another occasion to plan the celebration together, to invite all the family, and to share with the church family an important event in the young person's spiritual journey. I feel a little sad when confirmation candidates and their family do not stay for the usual cup of tea after the service but dash off to have their own private celebration. Try to plan the event so that you all have time to celebrate with the church family and allow them time to congratulate the young person and make a fuss of them before you leave to continue the celebration within the family. Don't stop celebrating the baptism just because they are confirmed. Baptism still remains important to the child and to the church; now you can add confirmation to the list of things to celebrate, and the baptism candle can be lit to remember that we still are to be a light in the world.

General

Between baptism and confirmation a great many things will happen to the child – first day at nursery or playgroup, first day at primary school, moving up the classes, a new sister or brother arriving, first encounter with death, first visit to hospital, and so on. The key words in all these situations are, once again, PREPARATION, SHARING, and PRAYER (PSP).

Preparation involves preparing yourself as anything affecting your child affects you; so think about the change that is about to happen, talk to friends who have already been through it, find out all you can about what is to happen, and commit yourself, your child and the situation to God in prayer. Then you can prepare your child, make preparations together, talk about what is going to happen. Explain in simple terms to the child – be honest with them about unpleasant things without getting into gory details.

Bereavement

Death has a tendency to come on us suddenly and there is little time for preparation, but sharing and prayer are essential. Do not hide your grief from the children. Share it with them – yes, it will upset them but they need to know how much you cared for the person who has died. If you hide your grief they may think you don't care and then they have to hide their grief, and their feelings get all confused and they can't talk about it. Talk to them, cry with them, remember with them, make a book together about the person, look at photographs of them, write down all you can remember about them, the things they did, the stories they told, the way they were, what they enjoyed, what aggravated them. Enjoy the memories and cry a bit and laugh a bit. Say prayers for the person who has died, giving thanks for all that they were to you, and for yourselves that you may always remember them and that the sadness will go. The book will become a book of fond memories to be taken out on anniversaries connected with the deceased person, and a bit of family history for everyone in the future, making sure they are never forgotten.

You will need to think about life after death. Share this in simple terms with the children but again, be honest about what you believe, don't make up fairy stories; and if you are not able to answer some of the questions say you don't know but discuss the question with your clergy person and get them to talk to the children if necessary. Three lovely books which might help are *Water Bugs and Dragonflies*, *Badgers Parting Gifts* and, for pets, *I'll Always Love You*.

Remember also that the death of a pet is felt very deeply by children and may well be their first contact with death. Treat it sensitively; have a little funeral service burying the pet in a special corner in the garden with a little marker, say some prayers and commit the pet to God's love. This will be a big help when later a loved person dies.

Moving house

Moving house is very stressful for all the family, and involves the grief of saying goodbye to a very special place, and probably people as well. This is followed by the trauma of meeting new people and places, schools and jobs. Preparation, sharing and prayer are important for you all. Take photographs of the old house, visit the new one as often as possible or look at photographs of it. Talk about the move, when it is to happen, what you need to do beforehand, what you will do at the new house, and explain simply but carefully why you have to move. As far as possible let the children choose their room. If it is to be decorated let them help choose the decoration and where the furniture is to be put.

Try not to have a big clear out. If you can get everything into the new house, take it with you: it is enough to say goodbye to the house without having to say goodbye to some of your possessions as well. Have farewell parties, but especially take time to say goodbye to the house. When it is empty, walk all through together and say goodbye, touch the walls, windows, doors, and say a prayer for the house and for the new people who will move in.

It is traditional to leave a fire laid in the house when you leave it to welcome the new inhabitants, and wish them warmth and shelter. Perhaps you could gather round that fireplace and say a final prayer for the house and the new occupants. Not every house has a fireplace these days of course, so you may have to think of another place, perhaps in the kitchen or by the door as you go out. Whether or not you are able to leave a fire laid, why not leave behind a note of welcome saying that you prayed for the house and for them and hope they will find peace and happiness in their new home and maybe leave a cross hanging somewhere? You never know what seeds you may be planting.

And so on to the new house – a new adventure, exciting and a little scary. Find some good things about the new house. Unfortunately there will probably be a few hiccups when you move, so try to play these down and make fun of them. Remember to give time to the children as well as rushing about to get the house straight. The important thing is not the building, nor the belongings, nor whether it is tidy and things are in their right place, but you and the family are what makes a home.

Talk about the move, reminisce and laugh about it, and arrange a house warming party soon, so that the extended family and friends old and new can come and visit and celebrate the move. Also, have the house blessed by your clergy person. This may be the same person as in the old house so s/he could help your prayers on leaving one and arriving at the other, or it may be a new person. It would help if you could meet the new person before the move and see if they would do a blessing. But you can do it yourself: there is a form of service in *Caught and Taught* available from Southwark Diocesan Board of Education (see Resource list).

Family milestones

There are lots of events which are important in the family which need marking in smaller ways, but the formula PREPARATION, SHARING and PRAYER (PSP) will fit them all. Exam results are pretty traumatic, especially when it means getting that place at college or not. Prepare yourself for this, how you will celebrate success and comfort failure. Share your thoughts with the person involved and prepare a little surprise that will fit either outcome. Pray about it and commit it to God's care. Going to college, leaving college, starting the first job, passing or failing the driving test, and so on are all milestones which need our love and support as parents and the knowledge that God is with us in all things.

A smashing little book to guide you on these milestones is called *Milestones*, published by Methodist Church Division of Education and Youth. It is written very simply and gives simple thoughts and guidance.

Church festivals

As well as milestones in our own lives we can celebrate milestones in the church's year. *Christmas* is an obvious one and you probably have developed little rituals about what you do on Christmas Day, who you share it with, when the presents are opened, which service you attend at church. Advent will have been full of preparations at home and in church and many people who are not committed Christians will celebrate the festival and even attend church.

Think about how you will keep the religious significance alive at home. Some things are very simple: the star on the top of the Christmas tree; a crib scene in a prominent place, perhaps small crib scenes in the children's bedrooms; an advent calendar which is based on the Christmas story; choosing cards which are religiously relevant to the story, not just Victorian snow scenes; including presents with a Christian flavour, such as books of Bible stories, prayer cards, Christian symbols to put in their room (not instead of, of course, but little additions to the normal presents); a table centre of Christmas roses and candles, and so on. The crib scene could be used to build up the Christmas story. Start about a week before Christmas with the stable on one side of the room and Mary and Joseph on the other side of the room. Each day move Mary and Joseph a little nearer the stable, arriving at the stable on the morning of Christmas Eve. During the night put the baby Jesus in the crib in the stable so he is found there on Christmas morning, when you can add the shepherds and put the three kings on the other side of the room. Move the kings a little closer each day so that they arrive on Epiphany Sunday. *The Lion Christmas Book* would give you some more ideas, and stories, and explanations of various Christmas traditions.

Easter is another obvious celebration and again you will probably have already established certain traditions. Lamb is the traditional meat for the Easter meal, and you may share it with friends and family. The main Easter service is communion, and you may be involved in services on Maundy Thursday, Good Friday, and perhaps in helping to decorate the church on Saturday, when the children may be involved in making the Easter garden. You may like to make an Easter garden at home on Good Friday. Easter eggs and chicks and baby rabbits are all part of the story symbolising the new life in Christ. Lion also produce *The Easter Book* full of stories, ideas and things to do.

And, of course, we must not forget *Mothering Sunday*! Ideas for that are in *The Easter Book* and also in a little book called *We always put a Candle in the Window* by Marjorie Freeman (see Resource list). This invaluable book has ideas for celebrating festivals in every month of the year such as Twelfth Night, St Valentine, Shrove Tuesday and Ash Wednesday, Mothering Sunday and Easter Weekend, Pentecost, Midsummer Day, Harvest, Advent and Christmas and even the anniversaries of birthdays, baptisms, confirmations, weddings and deaths. The ideas are simple and easy to do.

10
The church can help too!

Involving the families

Praying Samuels come from praying Hannahs, and praying leaders come from praying homes. First and most important is to make your church *welcoming to families*. If your building is very old and very traditional, this is not easy but with careful thought it's surprising what you can do. One very old church I know has converted the room at the bottom of the tower into toilets, including one for the disabled, and a kitchen. Where children are welcome it is important to have toilets and baby changing facilities.

In other churches a fairly large area has been cleared and carpeted where the small children can go and play with 'non-noisy' toys if they get bored in the service. This is better at the front of the church to one side as the children are then still very much part of the service and can easily be seen by Mum or Dad so they don't worry about them and can intervene in the play if necessary. Encourage families to sit at the front so the children can toddle off and play and return to Mum or Dad as and when they want. It is also easier to collect them when going up to the communion rail for a blessing. Psychologically it also says something about the church valuing and accepting the children just as they are; they are not being shut out at the back of the church or taken out to another room somewhere. They and their families are welcome and accepted because thoughtful provision has been made for them. 'Wriggle bags' are another good idea. These are simple draw-string bags filled with quiet toys, books, pictures to colour and crayons, etc. Parents are given the bags as they come into church 'to give to the little one if s/he gets bored'. The parents can then hand over the bag at an appropriate time and the child stays with Mum and Dad as a family. This avoids children bringing unsuitable noisy toys into church and helps if it is not possible to make a carpeted area.

Involve families in the service, carrying up the elements, reading the lesson from the dramatised Bible, doing the intercessions together, helping to serve the tea and coffee, not forgetting the soft drinks and children's biscuits (they don't go for Rich Tea much!), welcoming people at the door and giving out books – being welcomed by a family at the door will reassure other families that they are welcome.

Do everything you can to *make the church light and bright and warm* – not only children appreciate this! This is especially important at child height – try 'walking' round your church on your hands and knees to get an idea of what it looks like to a child!! Can children, the elderly and the handicapped gain access to your church or are the doors too heavy for them to open, the steps too high? Are the service books too heavy and cumbersome for small or arthritic hands to hold? Is the lighting too poor for old eyes to read by? Is coming to your church a fun outing to meet with friendly people? It takes a lot of courage to come to church with a young family these days, especially if you are new to church, perhaps coming before and after a baptism. If it is fun you may come again, if it is an ordeal you won't!

Baptism procedures

Baptism preparation and follow up are important not only to the families but also to the church. Baptism is a meeting point between the church and the family, whether they are regular church attenders or not and presents the church with a good opportunity to evangelise at a time when families need support. The church should encourage photographs to be taken, before and after the service, to include the clergy person who officiated. You might like to think about what would make good photographs: around the font, on the chancel steps so they get a view of the interior of the church and at the church door? Suggestions could be put on a leaflet which explains the service and what is expected of the family, to be given to the family before the service. Don't forget to involve the whole family in the baptism preparation, especially the other children who will not remember their own baptism and may feel put out when all the fuss is being made of the baby. Have you a policy about videos? Would you allow the whole service to be filmed? Put this policy in the leaflet also.

It is usual now to give a candle at the appropriate point in the service, but you can also buy attractive cards for the parents and godparents to remind them of their duties and the date of the baptism. It is also becoming common practice to do the welcome in the next Family

Service if the baptism has been private. This overcomes the difficulty of large baptism parties overwhelming the normal congregation on a Sunday, but still gives the congregation an opportunity to see and welcome the new member of the congregation, and to make the parents feel welcome in the church.

How about having a cradle roll, on the same lines as a Book of Remembrance, and include the children in the prayers on Sunday? It is a good idea to send cards on the child's birthday and baptism anniversary, and encourage the family to come to church to the Family Service nearest to the baptism anniversary and to add something in the prayers that day. Many churches have a church sponsor who is involved in the preparation, makes the promises with the godparents, and then keeps in touch with the baby, sending the cards, visiting occasionally, letting the parents know what is available at church for them and the children and, at the appropriate age inviting the child to Sunday School and encouraging the parents to come to Family Worship.

It is important that once having encouraged the parents to have the child baptised and to make the promises, the church then gives them appropriate opportunities for keeping those promises, such as Pram Services, Mums and Toddlers groups, Family Worship, Children's clubs, and so on.

Confirmation

As I noted in the previous chapter, it saddens me when the family of confirmation candidates rush off after the service to their own private celebration. Make it clear to parents that the whole congregation wants to join the celebration and congratulate the candidates, as well as appreciating that the event is a good excuse for a family gathering. You will therefore need to arrange the service at a time which allows the family to celebrate with the church family as well as having their own celebration. It is again important to involve the parents and siblings in the preparation so they know what is happening, and if possible talk to godparents and invite them to the service.

Confirmation should not be a graduation out of the church but a graduation into the church. Talk about this to both parents and candidates and again find opportunities for the young person and their family to develop their commitment in the context of the church family. You might have a follow-up club for the young people, and the whole family can be involved in Family Worship. There are various jobs in the church which might encourage the young people, choir, serving, music group, sidesperson, and so on. For older confirmands prayer groups and Bible study groups are a possibility, especially if prayer and Bible study have been part of the preparation.

If your confirmation or baptism policy needs reviewing, contact the Youth and Children's Advisers in your diocese who will be able to help and advise, and take a good look at the Synod Report *On the Way*.

Parenting

Parenting is not easy today, I don't think it ever has been, but the church can help by putting on parenting groups. You should have a FLAME representative in your diocese who can help you to do this, or you could do it yourself using the Veritas Parenting Programmes which are excellent (see Resource list). Just meeting together with other parents with children of similar ages is a great support. Sometimes parents think they are the only ones who have trouble with their children and it is good to know that everyone has these problems and to talk about how to cope with them – as well as to share the pleasures of parenthood.

There is not so much material to help with the spiritual life of families, and I hope this little book will be a contribution to this. However, there is no reason why you could not bring groups of families together to think of ways in which to practise their faith at home, giving them the opportunity to try things out and talk about the success or failure of the idea within the group. This gives a sense of security, and they are not battling on, on their own, struggling to find a way of living a Christian family life. Prayer groups and Bible study groups will give support to families in that they can help individuals in the family to develop their own private prayer and Bible study, and these need not be confined to adults. Why not have all-age groups, or prayer groups for teenagers and children? You might like to use David Durston's book *Faith in the Family* with a group of parents.

Bookstall

Some churches have a bookstall in church which encourages people to read Christian books, especially if there are few local Christian book-shops, and makes a little profit for the church funds at the same time. If you already have a bookstall make sure it includes books suitable for all ages. There are such good books now for children and teenagers it is a pity to leave them out. The younger the people start to read Christian books the better and it will hopefully become a habit for life.

Even better perhaps is a library so that people can borrow books for themselves and the family. Books are expensive today and a library will meet the need for frequent changes of books which the cost of pur-chase may preclude. You could also build up a number of music tapes for people to borrow – a good way of encouraging the learning of new songs, and new styles of music. There are some excellent videos avail-able today and if you could set up a video library as well this would be a wonderful way to communicate with a video generation. Remember there are videos to use in baptism and marriage preparation as well.

As well as a stall selling books, why not add some of the things I have suggested in this book like prayer cards, crosses and crucifix, posters, car stickers, lapel badges and so on? This would save families having to hunt around for these things, would encourage families to buy and use them in the home, and make a little profit for the church at the same time.

Prayer board in the church

How about putting a prayer board at the back of church to encourage people to pray about the needs around them and their individual needs? It is a good information board for the clergy and people, letting you know who is ill or in distress, reminding you of milestones in people's lives from school exams to Golden Weddings. You may wish to put candles and holders by it so that candles can be lit for the people on the board. The board can then be used in the intercessions, either by carrying the whole board down to the front of the church and reading from it or by making notes of what is on there.

Outings

It is good for families to have days out, either just for fun or for fun and fellowship, and this applies just as much to the church family as to the nuclear family. Some events are costly to attend as a small family but much cheaper for large parties. Some people both young and old do not drive or do not drive long distances. The church could organise family days – a parish picnic at a local beauty spot, a Christian concert or event, a trip to a pantomime at Christmas, a day outing to a theme park or farm museum or whatever is in your area, a retreat weekend or going to Spring Harvest. You might have a committee of young parents who could arrange these sort of things for the whole church family.

Appendix
The grace cube

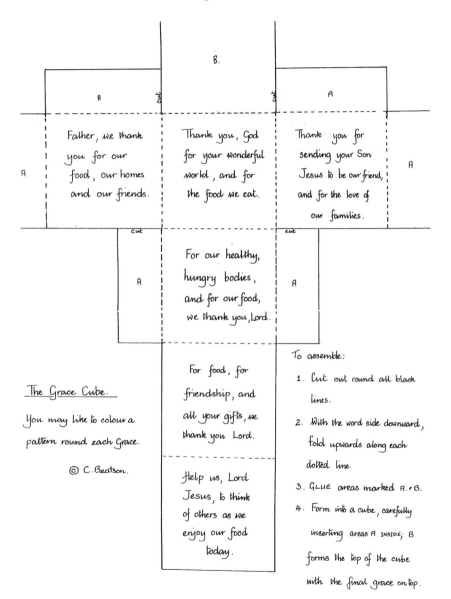

B.

A   out   cut   A

A

Father, we thank you for our food, our homes and our friends.

Thank you, God for your wonderful world, and for the food we eat.

Thank you for sending your Son Jesus to be our friend, and for the love of our families.

A

cut   cut

A

For our healthy, hungry bodies, and for our food, we thank you, Lord.

A

The Grace Cube.

You may like to colour a pattern round each Grace.

© C. Beatson.

For food, for friendship, and all your gifts, we thank you Lord.

Help us, Lord Jesus, to think of others as we enjoy our food today.

To assemble:

1. Cut out round all black lines.

2. With the word side downward, fold upwards along each dotted line.

3. GLUE areas marked A.&B.

4. Form into a cube, carefully inserting areas A INSIDE; B forms the top of the cube with the final grace on top.

91

Resource list

Addresses of suppliers of prayer cards, videos, etc.

Christian Art

Kingsway Communications Ltd	UNICEF	Vanpoules
Lottbridge Drove	25 Churchgate	101d Lodge Lane
Eastbourne	Leicester	Purley
Sussex BN23 6NT	LE1 3AL	Surrey CR8 4DG

Prayer cards

Tim Tiley Prints	Palm Tree Press/Kevin Mayhew
Eblana Lodge	Rattlesden
157 Cheltenham Rd	Bury St Edmunds
Bristol BS6 5RR	Suffolk IP30 0SZ

Videos

Scripture Union	CPAS (Hippity Dog series)	CTVC
9–11 Clothier Road	Athena Drive	Hillside
Bristol BS4 5RL	Tachbrook Park	Merry Hill Rd
	Warwick CV34 6NG	Bushey
		Watford
		Herts WD2 1DR

Scripture Press Foundation Ltd.	Look and Listen Library Ministries
Raans Road	01895 624774
Amersham-on-the-Hill	(They will lend you videos to start
Bucks HP6 6LQ	a library in your church.)

Tape

A. Ashwin, *Patterns in Prayer*, Eagle, 1992.

Books

Angela Ashwin, *Exploring Prayer: Patterns not Padlocks. Prayer for Parents of Young Children*, Eagle, 1992.

Simon Bailey, *Stations: Places for Pilgrims to Pray*, Cairns Publications, 1991.

N. Beilenson, *Table Graces*, Lutterworth, 1987.

Michael Botting, *Prayers for All the Family*, Kingsway, 1993.

Caught and Taught, Southwark Diocesan Board of Education, 48 Union Street, London SE1 1TD, 1993.

Peter Churchill, *Feeling Good: Songs of Wonder and Worship for Fives and Under*, Church House Publishing, 1994.

David Durston, *Faith in the Family*, Bible Society, 1991.

The Essential Christmas Book, Lion Publishing, 1994.

The Essential Easter Book, Lion Publishing, 1996.

M. Forster, *A Story, A Hug and A Prayer*, Kevin Mayhew, 1994.

M. Freeman, *We Always Put a Candle in the Window*, Church House Publishing, 1989.

C. E. Hall *et al.*, *Milestones: Marking Important Events for Children and Parents*, Methodist Church Division of Education and Youth, 1993.

E. Laird, *Grace for Children*, HarperCollins, 1989.

The Lion Book of Children's Prayers, Lion Publishing, 1977.

R. Makeler, *Grace after Meals*, Stewart, 1985.

C. Martin, *A Book of Graces*, Hodder and Stoughton, 1992.

On the Way: Towards an Integrated Approach to Christian Initiation, Church House Publishing, 1995.

L. and D. Osborn, *Celebrating Families*, SPCK, 1995.

Palm Tree Books (e.g. Bible Quizzes, Bible cut-outs), Palm Tree Press,

Rattlesden, Bury St Edmonds.

S. Sayers, *Including Children*, Kevin Mayhew, 1990.

Susan Varley, *Badger's Parting Gifts*, Collins, 1992.

Veritas Parenting Programmes, Family Caring Trust, 44 Rathfriland Rd, Newry, Co Down BT34 1LD.

Doris Stickney, *Water Bugs and Dragonflies*, Mowbray, 1982.

Hans Wilhelm, *I'll Always Love You*, Hodder and Stoughton, 1991.

Magazines

Bible Stories, magazine, Redan Co. Ltd, Appleton House, 139 King Street, London W6 9JG, price £1.10 or annual subscription of £5.97.

Time for the Family, Scripture Union magazine, 9–11 Clothier Road, Bristol BS4 5RL.

The Vision, magazine, Journal of the National Retreat Association, Central Hall, 256 Bermondsey St, London SE1 3UJ, price £3.50.

Parentwise, monthly magazine for parents, Elm House, 37 Elm Road, New Malden, Surrey KT3 3HB, price £1.70.

If you would like to visit the annual Christian Resources Exhibition, where many firms display their goods and you can see before you buy, ring 01844-342894 for information on your nearest exhibition. For a Bible Reading Fellowship catalogue, write to:

The Bible Reading Fellowship
Peter's Way
Sandy Lane West
Oxford OX4 5HG

Index